IN THE
Presence
OF HIS
Majesty

OSWALD
CHAMBERS

MULTNOMAH BOOKS
SISTERS, OREGON

Introduction

When Oswald Chambers died, a telegram was sent by his wife stating simply...

Oswald in His presence.

What a prospect to be in the presence of His majesty! In this life, we must be content with only glimpses of the Lord's presence. Perhaps they occur during personal devotions, while observing God's creation, or as we sit in church worshipping with other believers. Sometimes they are in the common happenings of life. Discovering Him in everyday life deepens when we are purposefully *practicing His presence*.

This was the goal of Oswald Chambers—a life centered on the ever-increasing enjoyment of God's presence. No wonder one cannot read his words without being revitalized by his driving passion for Christ. His spiritual antennae constantly received signals from the Master. Oswald learned obedience and trust by faith, which resulted in love, humility, worship, and hope. His entire life became a reflection of the apostle Paul's words:

Therefore having been justified by faith,

we have peace with God through our Lord Jesus Christ,

through whom also we have obtained our introduction by faith

into this grace in which we stand;

and we exalt in hope of the glory of God.

And not only this, but we also exult in our tribulations,

knowing that tribulation brings about perseverance;

and perseverance, proven character;

and proven character, hope;

and hope does not disappoint, because the love of God

has been poured out within our hearts

through the Holy Spirit who was given to us.

ROMANS 5:1–5, NAS

The devotional thoughts in this book have been carefully arranged in three sections. For each section, I've written brief introductory comments to help you practice the presence of God in your life—a journey that will yield increasing *faith*, glorious *hope*, and immeasurable *love*.

And now abide faith, hope, and love, these three;

but the greatest of these is love.

1 Corinthians 13:13, NKJ

John Van Diest

Associate Publisher

Faith

Faith

Faith

What a powerful word! Faith is the cornerstone of a person's relationship with God—pivotal in pleasing God and necessary to experience His saving grace. It is by faith that we are reconciled and can enjoy peace with Him.

Faith

is always personal. A life of faith is based on a growing trust in God as He reveals Himself in His Word. Faith often defies ordinary common sense, for faith is a spiritual exercise and common sense is a natural exercise. Since faith is personal, it is developed through testing and trials often disguised as "circumstances." God's purpose in designing or allowing these difficulties is to educate our faith and make Jesus very real to us. "Until we know Jesus, God is merely a concept...," writes Chambers. "Faith is the entire person in the right relationship with God through the power of the Spirit of Jesus Christ."

Faith

The writer of Hebrews defines faith as "the assurance of things hoped for, the conviction of things not seen." Following this powerful definition are examples of men and women who by their faith accomplished what God intended (Hebrews 11). It's like reading a biblical *Who's Who*. Had Oswald Chambers lived during Bible times, he most likely would have been included in this list of "faith heroes." One thing is certain—Chambers believed God. Faith was the *modus operandi* of his whole life. –JVD

Faith that is sure of itself is not faith....
Faith that is sure of God is the only faith there is.

Oswald Chambers

Faith

To understand the tiniest bit of truth about God is to love it with all our heart and soul and mind; all that lies dark and obscure just now, is one day going to be as clear, as radiantly and joyously clear, as the bit we have seen. Have faith!

Faith

The great need is not to *do* things, but to *believe* things.
The Redemption of Christ is not an experience, it is the great
act of God which He has performed through Christ,
and I have to build my faith upon it.

Faith is more than an attitude of mind, faith is the complete,
passionate, earnest trust of our whole nature in the Gospel
of God's grace as it is presented in the Life and Death
and Resurrection of our Lord Jesus Christ.

Faith is not intelligent understanding; faith is deliberate
commitment to a Person where I see no way.

If we have faith at all it must be faith in Almighty God;
when He has said a thing, He will perform it; we have
to remain steadfastly obedient to Him.

In the Presence of His Majesty

Faith

There is nothing so secure as the salvation of God; it is as eternal as the mountains, and it is our trust in God that brings us the conscious realization of this.

If a man will resign himself in implicit trust to the Lord Jesus, he will find that He leads the wayfaring soul into the green pastures and beside the still waters, so that even when he goes through the dark valley of the shadow of some staggering episode, he will fear no evil. Nothing in life or death, time or eternity, can stagger a soul from the certainty of the Way, for one moment.

A man can never be the same again, I don't care who he is, after having heard Jesus Christ preached. He may say he pays no attention to it; he may appear to have forgotten all about it, but he is never quite the same, and at any moment trust may spring up into his consciousness that will destroy all his peace and happiness.

*N*othing has any power to alter a man save the incoming of the life of Jesus, and that is the only sign that he is born again.

*T*hrough the Redemption, God undertakes to deal with a man's past, and He does it in two ways: by forgiving him, and by making the past a wonderful culture for the future.

Faith

*T*he center of salvation is the Cross, and why it is so easy to be saved is because it cost God so much.

*W*hen a so-called rationalist points out sin and iniquity and disease and death, and he says "How does God answer that?" you have always a fathomless answer—the Cross of Christ.

Faith

Belief must be the *will* to believe. There must be a surrender of the will, not a surrender to persuasive power, but a deliberate launching forth on God, and on what He says, until I am no longer confident in what I have done, I am only confident in God. The hindrance is that I will not trust God, but only my mental understanding.

When we have a certain belief, we kill God in our lives, because we do not believe Him, we believe our beliefs about Him....

Believe what you saw when you were in the light, and when you are in the plowed field and God's moral seasons are going over you—the remainder of the cold, hard winter, the beginnings of the strange, painful stirrings of spring—keep abandoned to Him. He knows the seasons to bring to your soul as He does in the natural world.

Faith

*J*esus Christ is God incarnate coming into human flesh from the outside, His life is the Highest and the Holiest entering in at the lowliest door. Have I allowed my personal life to become a "Bethlehem" for the Son of God?

How much of our security and peace is the outcome of the civilized life we live, and how much of it is built up in faith in God?

Unbelief is the most active thing on earth; it is a fretful, worrying, questioning, annoying, self-centered spirit. To believe is to stop all this and let God work.

Put all "supposing" on one side and dwell in the shadow of the Almighty. Deliberately tell God that you will not fret about that thing. All our fret and worry is caused by calculating without God.

We must strenuously cast our ways and our burdens on Him and wait for Him in all haphazard and topsy-turvy moments.

For we walk by faith, not by sight.
2 CORINTHIANS 5:7, NKJ

Faith

There are certain tempers of mind in which we never dare indulge. If we find they have distracted us from faith in God, then until we get back to the quiet mood before God, our faith in Him is nil, and our confidence in the flesh and human ingenuity is the thing that rules.

If you put your faith in your experience anything that happens—toothache, indigestion, an east wind, uncongenial work—is likely to upset the experience, but nothing that happens can ever upset God or the almighty reality of the Redemption; once based on that, you are as eternally sure as God Himself.

When we are standing face to face with Jesus and He says "Believest thou this?" our faith is as natural as breathing, and we say— "Yes Lord," and are staggered and amazed that we were so stupid as not to trust Him before.

This is the victory that has overcome the world...our faith.

1 JOHN 5:4, NIV

Hope

Hope

Hope

is one of God's great abiding truths. Psalm 147 teaches us that God takes pleasure in those who hope in His unwavering love and in those who fear Him. We fear Him because of His great power, but our hope still rests in Him because of His indescribable magnificence—and God is delighted by both!

Hope

is a noun—it is something we come to know. *Hope* is a verb—it is something we do.

Scripture is resplendent with words of hope. Here are only a few thoughts gleaned from the New Testament: having hope in something we already see is not really hope at all. Rather, our hope in God and His promises grows with our understanding of His word, producing a pure spirit and pure living. That hope, expressed in love, causes us to rejoice and look forward to the coming glory, which in turn makes us bold in the present. Ultimately, hope will not disappoint us.

C.S. Lewis wrote:

Hope...means a continual looking forward to the eternal world....

Aim at heaven and you will get earth "thrown in."

Aim at earth and you will get neither....

As you read these words on hope, lift your face toward the light of His
glory and you will find yourself smiling as you embrace the future. –JVD

Hope

To trust in the Lord is to be foolish enough to know that if we fulfill God's commands, He will look after everything.

That we may know what is the hope of His calling—have I allowed my mind to get stagnant about Jesus Christ's hope and taken another aim for my life? Sooner or later we must come, either with a sense of havoc or a sense of rejoicing, to Jesus Christ's standard for us.

Every time you venture out in the life of faith you will find something in your common sense cares that flatly contradicts your faith. Can you trust Jesus Christ where your common sense cannot trust Him?

Be strong, and let your heart take courage,

All you who hope in the Lord.

PSALM 31:24, NAS

Hope

"Why does God bring thunderclouds and disasters when we want green pastures and still waters?" Bit by bit we find, behind the clouds, the Father's feet; behind the lightning, an abiding day that has no night; behind the thunder, "a still small voice" that comforts with a comfort that is unspeakable.

The whole claim of the Redemption of Jesus is that He can satisfy the last aching abyss of the human soul, not only hereafter, but here and now.

Hope

*H*ow many of us get into a panic when we are faced by physical desolation, by death, or war, injustice, poverty, disease? All these in all their force will never turn to panic the one who believes in the absolute sovereignty of his Lord.

*T*he thing that preserves a man from panic is his relationship to God; if he is only related to himself and to his own courage, there may come a moment when his courage gives out.

*D*on't be disturbed today by thoughts about tomorrow; leave tomorrow alone, and bank in confidence on God's organizing of what you do not see.

We have this hope as an anchor for the soul,

firm and secure.

HEBREWS 6:19, NIV

There are disasters to be faced by the one who is in real fellowship with the Lord Jesus Christ. God has never promised to keep us immune from trouble; He says, "I will be with him in trouble," which is a very different thing.

What we call crises, God ignores, and what God reveals as the great critical moments of a man's life we look on as humdrum commonplaces. When we become spiritual we discern that God was in the humdrum commonplace and we never knew it.

Notion your mind with the idea that God is there. Nothing happens in any particular unless God's will is behind it, therefore you can rest in perfect confidence in Him.

God is never away off somewhere else; He is always *there*.

Hope

In our own spiritual experience some terror comes down the road to meet us and our hearts are seized with a tremendous fear; then we hear our own name called, and the voice of Jesus saying, "It is I, be not afraid," and the peace of God which passeth all understanding takes possession of our hearts.

Experiences of what God has done for me are only stepping-stones; the one great note is—I trust in the Lord Jesus, God's providence can do with me what it likes, make the heavens like brass, earth like hell, my body loathsome (as Job's was), but the soul that is trusting in Jesus gets where Job got, "Though He slay me, yet will I trust Him."

Who of us can see, behind chance and in chance, God? Who of us can see the finger of God in the weather? When we are in living touch with God we begin to discern that nothing happens by chance.

It does not matter where a man may get to in the way of tribulation or anguish, none of it can wedge in between and separate him from the love of God in Christ Jesus.

No matter what our circumstances are, we can be as sure of abiding in Him in them as in a prayer meeting.

A great point is reached spiritually when we stop worrying God over personal matters or over any matter. God expects of us the one thing that glorifies Him—and that is to remain absolutely confident in Him, remembering what He has said beforehand, and sure that His purpose will be fulfilled.

*G*od grant we may get to the place where discouragement is as impossible to us as it was to the Lord Jesus. The one dominant note of His life was the doing of His Father's will.

He only is my rock and my salvation (Psalm 62:6). A rock conveys the idea of an encircling guard, as that of a mother watching her child who is learning to walk; should the child fall, he falls into the encircling love and watchfulness of the mother's care.

The man who has seen Jesus can never be daunted; the man who has only a personal testimony as to what Jesus had done for him may be daunted, but nothing can turn the man who has seen Him; he endures "as seeing Him Who is invisible."

When by God's grace you become possessed of a new disposition, your nerves which have been used to obeying the wrong disposition are sure to say *"I can't"* and you must say *"You must,"* and to your amazement you find you can.

*J*esus Christ can put into the man, whose energy has been sapped by sin and wrong until he is all but in hell, a life so strong and full that Satan has to flee whenever he meets him. Jesus Christ can make any life more than conqueror as they draw on His Resurrection life.

Now may the God of hope fill you with all joy and peace in believing, that you may abound in hope by the power of the Holy Spirit.

ROMANS 15:13, NKJ

A river touches places of which its source knows nothing, and Jesus says if we have received of His fullness, however small the visible measure of our lives, out of us will flow rivers that will bless to the uttermost parts of the earth….

*G*od does not give us overcoming life: He gives life to the man who overcomes. In every case of tribulation, from gnats to the cruelty of the sword, we take the step as though there were no God to assist us, and we find He is there.

Can God keep me from stumbling this second? Yes. Can He keep me from sin this second? Yes. Well, that is the whole of life. You cannot live more than a second at a time. If God can keep you blameless this second, He can do it the next. No wonder Jesus Christ said "Let not your heart be troubled"! We do get troubled when we do not remember the amazing power of God.

Love

Love

Love

Who isn't interested in love? Henry Drummond wrote that it is "the greatest thing in the world." Yet few people know what love is—and even fewer experience real love in their lives.

The source of all love is God Himself—in fact, God is love. Love is so much a part of who He is that, should He cease to love, He would cease to be God. We can neither earn God's love nor lose His love.

Love

Richard C. Halverson described it this way:

> *God does not love some more than others.*
>
> *God does not love some less than others.*
>
> *God's love is unchanging—cannot be manipulated*
>
> * or exploited.*
>
> *God's love is universal—infinite—eternal—unlimited.*
>
> *God's love is personal—impartial—unconditional.*
>
> *God's love is forever!*
>
> *You can reject God's love. He will not make you, force*
>
> * you, or coerce you to accept His love!*

Since that is true, abiding in God's love becomes a treasured gift for every believer. –JVD

Love is not premeditated—it is spontaneous,
it bursts forth in extraordinary ways.
The evidence of our love for Him is the
absolute spontaneity of our love,
which flows directly from the nature within us.

Oswald Chambers
My Utmost for His Highest

Love

*I*n the Cross we may see the dimensions of Divine love. The Cross is not the cross of a man, but an exhibition of the heart of God. At the back of the wall of the world stands God with His arms outstretched, and every man driven there is driven into the arms of God. The Cross of Jesus is the supreme evidence of the love of God.

*G*od and love are synonymous. Love is not an attribute of God, it *is* God. Whatever God is, love is. If your conception of love does not agree with justice and judgment, purity and holiness, then your idea of love is wrong.

*T*he self-expenditure of the love of God exhibited in the life and death of our Lord becomes a bridge over the gulf of sin; human love can be imbued by Divine love, the love that never fails.

Whoever does not love does not know God, because God is love.

1 JOHN 4:8, NIV

*T*he springs of love are in God, that means they cannot be found anywhere else. It is absurd for us to try and find the love of God in our hearts naturally, it is not there any more than the life of Jesus Christ is there. Love and life are in God and in Jesus Christ and in the Holy Spirit whom God gives us, not because we merit Him, but according to His own particular graciousness.

When we know the love of Christ, which passeth knowledge, it means we are free from anxiety, free from carefulness, so that, during the twenty-four hours of the day, we do what we ought to do all the time, with the strength of life bubbling up with real spontaneous joy.

Perfect love casteth out fear, but to say "therefore will we not fear, though the earth be removed..." is only possible when the love of God is having its way.

Love

If I speak in the tongues of men and of angels, but have not love, I am only a resounding gong or a clanging cymbal. If I have the gift of prophecy and can fathom all mysteries and all knowledge, and if I have a faith that can move mountains, but have not love, I am nothing. If I give all I possess to the poor and surrender my body to the flames, but have not love, I gain nothing.

Love

Love is patient, love is kind. It does not envy, it does not boast, it is not
proud. It is not rude, it is not self-seeking, it is not easily angered, it keeps no
record of wrongs. Love does not delight in evil but rejoices with the truth. It
always protects, always trusts, always hopes, always perseveres.

L o v e

Love never fails. But where there are prophecies, they will cease; where there are tongues, they will be stilled; where there is knowledge, it will pass away. For we know in part and we prophesy in part, but when perfection comes, the imperfect disappears. When I was a child, I talked like a child, I thought like a child, I reasoned like a child. When I became a man, I put childish ways behind me. Now we see but a poor reflection as in a mirror; then we shall see face to face. Now I know in part; then I shall know fully, even as I am fully known.

And now these three remain: faith, hope, and love.
But the greatest of these is love.
1 CORINTHIANS 13, NAS

*L*ove never faileth!"*—What a wonderful phrase that is!

but what a still more wonderful thing the reality of that love must be;

> greater than prophecy—that vast forth-telling of the mind and
>> purpose of God;

> greater than the practical faith that can remove mountains;

> greater than philanthropic self-sacrifice;

> greater than the extraordinary gifts of emotions and ecstasies and
>> all eloquence;

> and it is this love that is shed abroad in our hearts by the Holy
>> Ghost which is given unto us.

*G*od has loved me to the end of all my sinfulness, of all my self-will, all my stiff-neckedness, all my pride, all my self-interest; now He says—"Love one another, as I have loved you." I am to show my fellow men the same love that God showed me. That is Christianity in practical working order.

Love

The love of God in Christ Jesus is such that He can take the most unfit man—unfit to survive, unfit to fight, unfit to face moral issues—and make him not only fit to survive and to fight, but fit to face the biggest moral issues and the strongest power of Satan, and come off more than conqueror.

My worth to God in public is what I am in private. Is my master ambition to please Him and be acceptable to Him, or is it something else, no matter how noble?

Love

It is the most natural thing to be like the person you live with most, therefore live most with Jesus Christ; be absorbingly taken up with Him.

Be simply and directly and unmistakably His today.

L o v e

We have to form the mind of Christ until we are absorbed with Him and take no account of the evil done to us. No love on earth can do this but only the love of God.

A self indwelt by Jesus becomes like Him. "Walk in love, even as Christ also loved you." Jesus has loved me to the end of all my meanness and selfishness and sin; now, He says, show that same love to others.

We have to love where we cannot respect and where we must not respect, and this can only be done on the basis of God's love for us.

> *My command is this: Love each other*
> *as I have loved you.*
> JOHN 15:12, NIV

IN THE PRESENCE OF HIS MAJESTY

published by Multnomah Books
a part of the Questar publishing family

© 1996 by Questar Publishers, Inc.

Edited by John Van Diest and Chip MacGregor
Design by Left Coast Design, Inc.
Portland, Oregon
Cover photo: Londie Padelsky
Interior photos: Steve Terrill

International Standard Book Number: 1-57673-125-1
Printed in Mexico

These selections from *Run Today's Race* by Oswald Chambers are published by special arrangement
with and permission of Discovery House Publishers, Box 3566, Grand Rapids, Michigan 49501.
Original copyright © 1968 by The Oswald Chambers Publications Association, Ltd.

Scripture quotations are from:
The Holy Bible, New International Version (NIV)
© 1973, 1984 by International Bible Society,
used by permission of Zondervan Publishing House

New American Standard Bible (NASB)
© 1960, 1977 by the Lockman Foundation

The New King James Version (NKJV)
© 1984 by Thomas Nelson, Inc.

For information:
Questar Publishers, Inc.
Post Office Box 1720
Sisters, Oregon 97759

96 97 98 99 00 01 02 03 — 11 10 9 8 7 6 5 4 3 2 1